Editor
Kim Fields

Editorial Project Manager
Mara Ellen Guckian

Editor-in-Chief
Sharon Coan, M.S. Ed.

Illustrators
Kelly McMahon
Kevin McCarthy

Cover Artist
Brenda DiAntonis

Art Manager
Kevin Barnes

Art Director
CJae Froshay

Imaging
Ralph Olmedo, Jr.
James Edward Grace

Product Manager
Phil Garcia

Publisher
Mary D. Smith, M.S. Ed.

Sort, , & Tally

Author

Amy DeCastro, M.A.

Teacher Created Resources, Inc.
6421 Industry Way
Westminster, CA 92683
www.teachercreated.com

ISBN: 978-0-7439-3390-2

©2003 Teacher Created Resources, Inc.
Reprinted, 2012
Made in U.S.A.

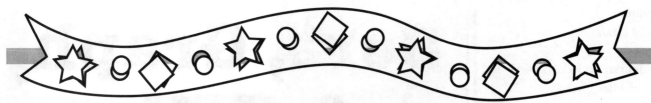

Table of Contents

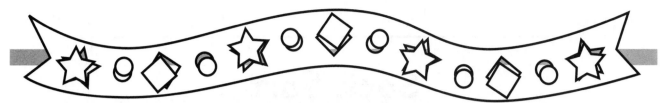

Introduction

Getting children ready for academic success starts in the earliest years. The early years pose special challenges because that is when children's attitudes toward school and learning are shaped. The purpose of the workbooks in this series is to promote children's development and learning and to make that journey a pleasant experience. Young children need a lot of repetition and directions that are simply worded. The activities that they are exposed to need to be enjoyable and visually stimulating. This series was developed with exactly that in mind. Each activity book was designed to introduce young learners to new concepts and review ones already learned. Through practice, children learn the many skills they will need for school and later life. This workbook includes practice in the following areas:

Sorting—Sorting activities encourage children to use critical thinking skills by comparing attributes of different objects or arrangements by size, color, shape, and quantity.

Graphing—Graphing activities help develop number sense and strategies for counting, comparing, and keeping track of quantities. Graphing also teaches children to collect, record, and represent data in a variety of ways.

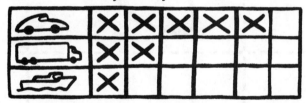

Tallying—Tallying activities help develop strategies for one-to-one correspondence, counting, and recording mathematical information. These skills go hand in hand to aid in the development of number and operation sense.

You will be delighted as you watch your students discover how interesting learning can be all year long with the gradual sequence of one page, easy-to-follow practice activities. They are great for enrichment, classroom practice, tutoring, home schooling, or just for fun.

With *Sort, Graph, & Tally,* young learners will gain the basic skills needed to become proficient mathematicians through reasoning, communicating, and problem solving.

Name _____

Sock Sort

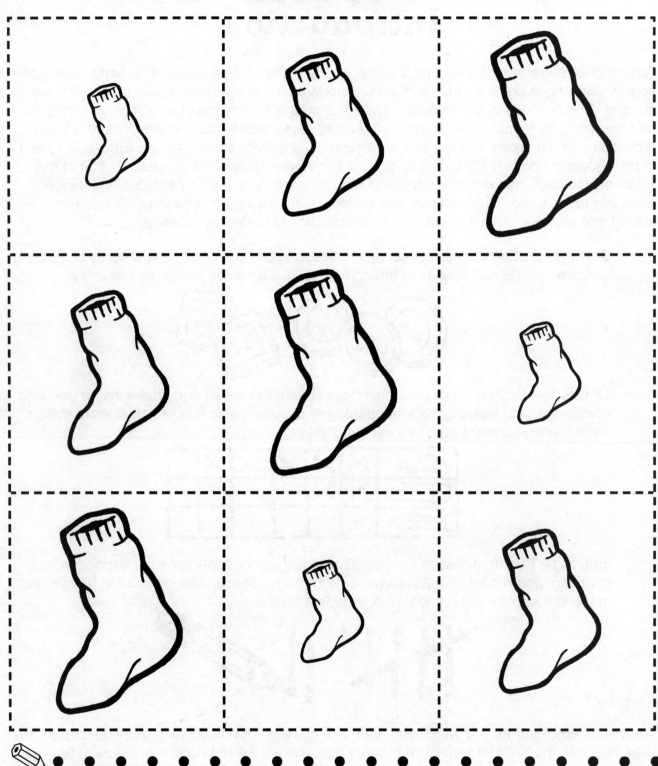

Directions: Cut out the socks. Sort the socks according to size.

Name _____

Shape Sort

Directions: Color the *small* shapes red. Color the *medium-sized* shapes yellow. Color the *large* shapes blue. Cut out the shapes and sort them according to size, then shape.

Name _____

Which Doesn't Belong?

Directions: Look at the items in each row. Put a big **X** on the item that doesn't belong.

Name _____

Food Sort

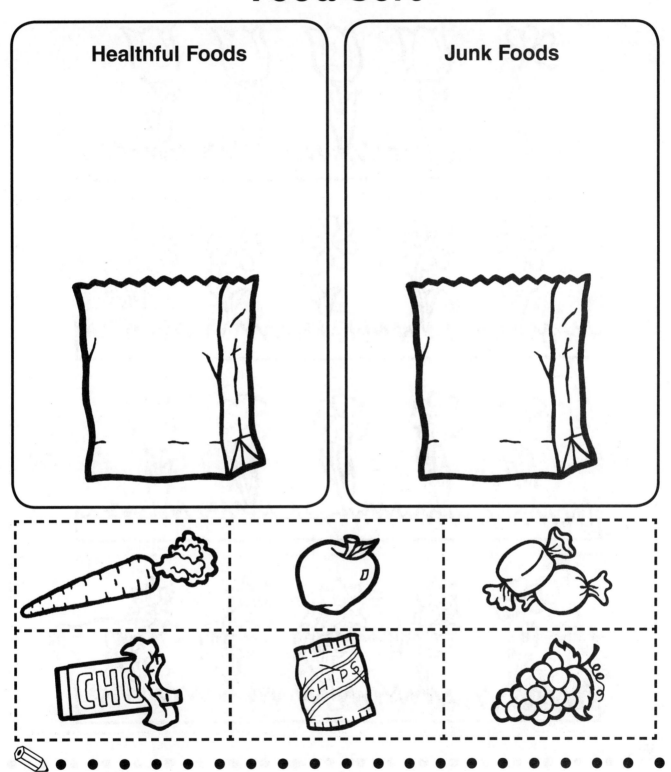

Healthful Foods	Junk Foods

Directions: Cut out the food items. Glue each food in the appropriate section.

Name _____

Flower Sort

● ● ● ● ● ● ● ● ● ● ● ● ● ● ● ● ● ● ● ●

Directions: Look at the flowers in each row. Color the flower that is *different* orange. Color the flowers that are the *same* red.

Name _____

Size Sort

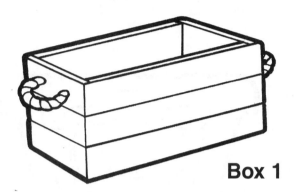

Box 1

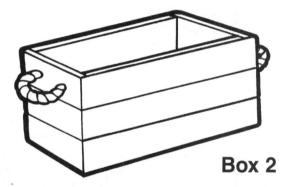

Box 2

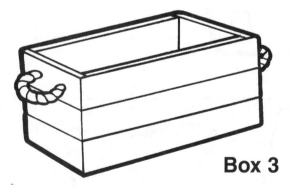

Box 3

Directions: Draw *small* balls in the first ball box. Draw *large* balls in the second ball box. Draw *medium-sized* balls in the third ball box.

Name _____

Put It Away!

Directions: Cut out the clothes. Glue each item on top of the appropriate basket.

Name _____

Tool Time

Directions: Put an **X** on the tools that belong in the *large* toolbox. Circle the tools that belong in the *small* toolbox.

Name _____

Home Sweet Home

Directions: Draw a line from each animal to its home.

Name _____

What To Wear?

Directions: Color the things that Amy would wear at the beach. Cross out the items that she would not wear at the beach.

Name _____

How Many Legs?

6 Legs	8 Legs

Directions: Cut out the bugs. Count the legs on each bug. Glue each bug in the appropriate box.

Name _____

Inside or Outside?

Direction: Draw a line from each inside item to the living room. Draw a line from each outside item to the tree.

Name _____

Land or Water?

Directions: Color the animals that live in the water blue. Color the animals that live on land brown.

Name _____

Button Sort

Directions: Cut out the buttons. Sort them according to size, shape, then number of holes.

Name _____

Book Sort

Directions: Draw a line from each book about an animal to the animal bookshelf. Draw a line from each book about food to the food bookshelf.

Name _____

Season Sort

Directions: Cut out each picture. Glue each summer item on the sandal. Glue each winter item on the boot.

19   #3390 Sort, Graph, & Tally

Pie Graph

Directions: Look at the pie. Color the *largest* section green. Color the *smallest* section red. Color the *medium-sized* section orange.

Name _____

Milk Carton Count

Chocolate Milk	Milk

- Which flavor of milk is the most popular? Color that column red.
- Which flavor of milk is the least popular? Color that column blue.
- Are there enough cartons for 7 children? Talk about your answer.

Directions: Look at the graph to answer the questions.

Name _____

Show and Tell

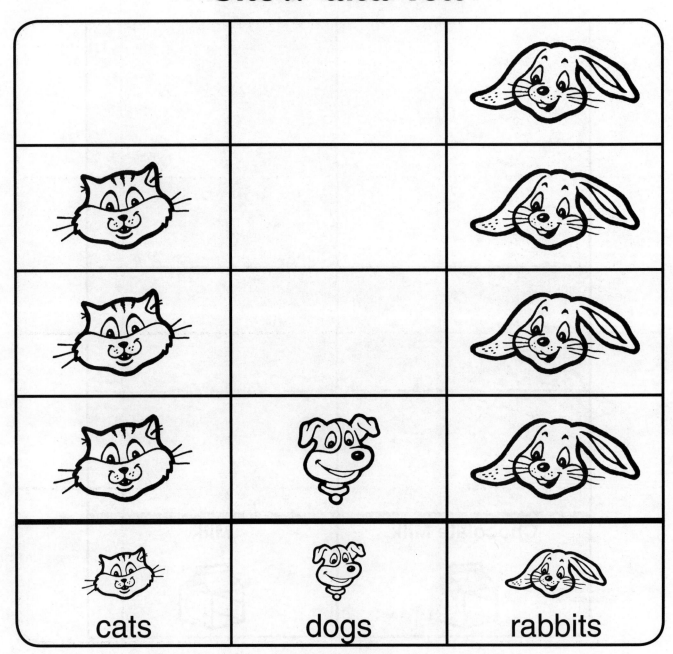

- Which animal was shown most often? Circle that column.
- Which animal was shown least often? Color that column blue.
- Which animal was shown 3 times? Color that column yellow.

Directions: Look at the graph to answer the questions.

Name _____

More or Less

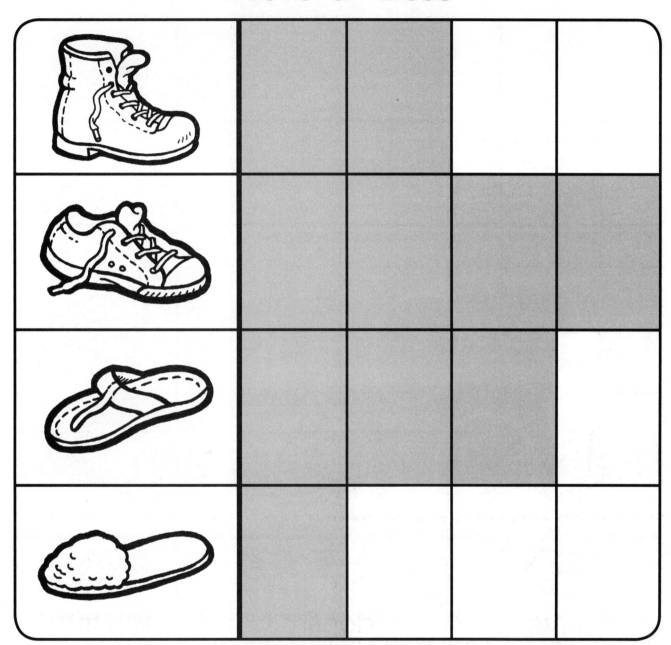

- Use blue to color the row that has the most shoes.
- Use yellow to color the row that has 2 shoes.
- Use red to color the row with the least amount of shoes.

Directions: Look at the graph to answer the questions.

Name _____

Favorite Holiday

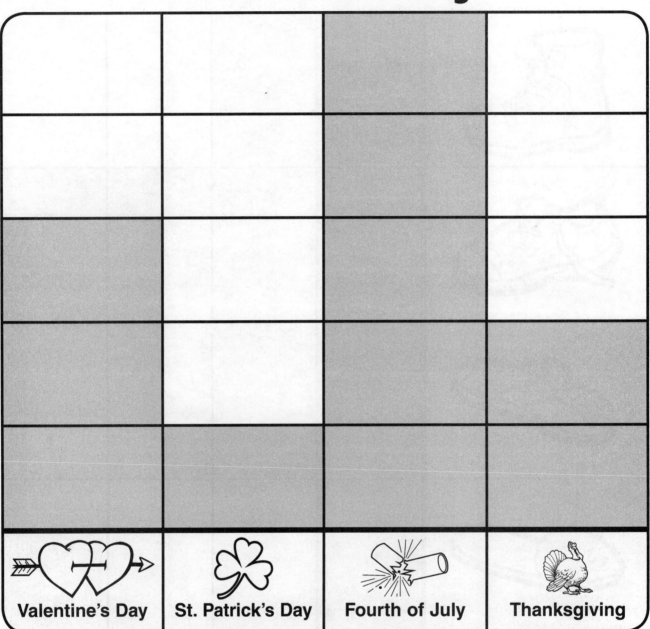

Valentine's Day	St. Patrick's Day	Fourth of July	Thanksgiving

- Which was the most popular holiday? Circle that column.
- Which was the least popular holiday? Put an **X** on that column.
- Which holiday did 3 children choose? Color that column red.

Directions: Look at the graph to answer the questions.

Name _____

Book Graph

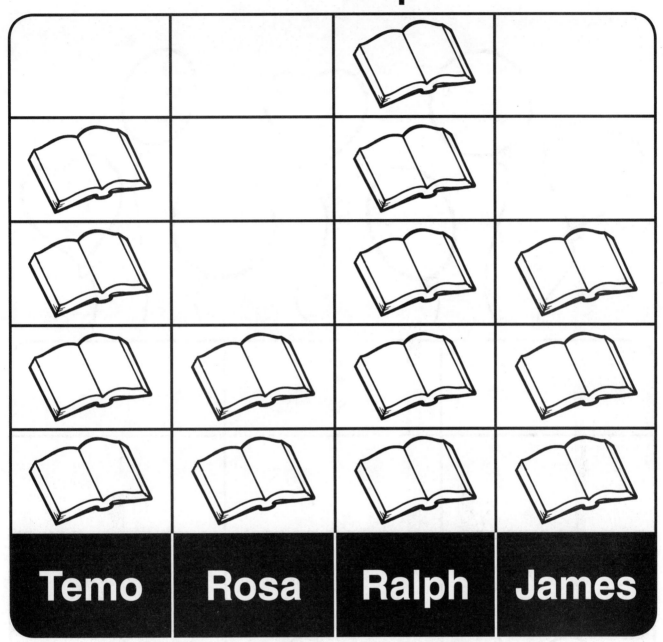

| Temo | Rosa | Ralph | James |

- Who read the most books? Color that column red.
- Who read the fewest books? Color that column yellow.
- Who read 4 books? Color that column green.

Directions: Look at the graph to answer the questions.

Name _____

Graph It!

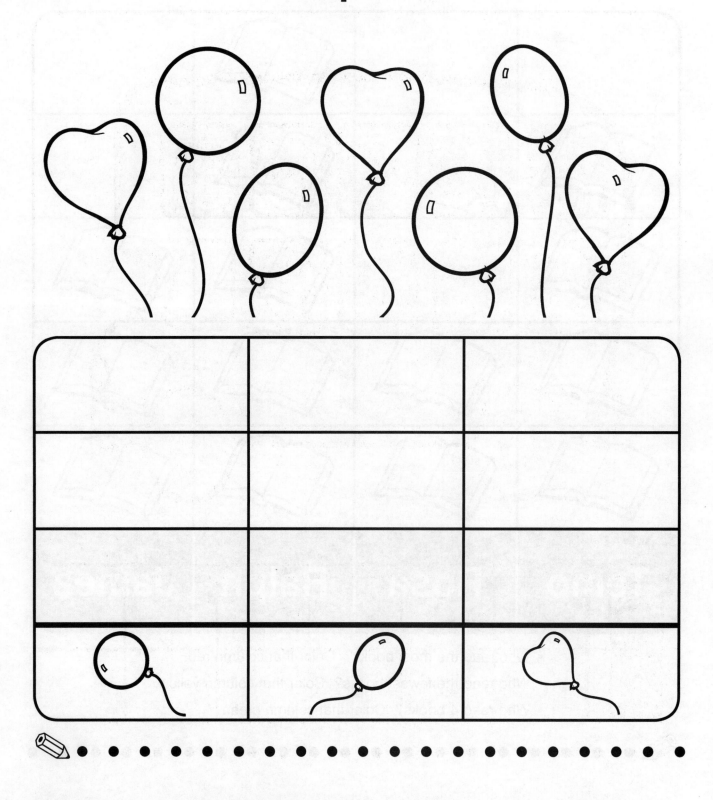

Directions: Count each type of balloon. Graph the total for each.

Name _____

Boys and Girls

Directions: Count each boy and girl on the bus. Graph the total for each.

Name _____

Who's Older?

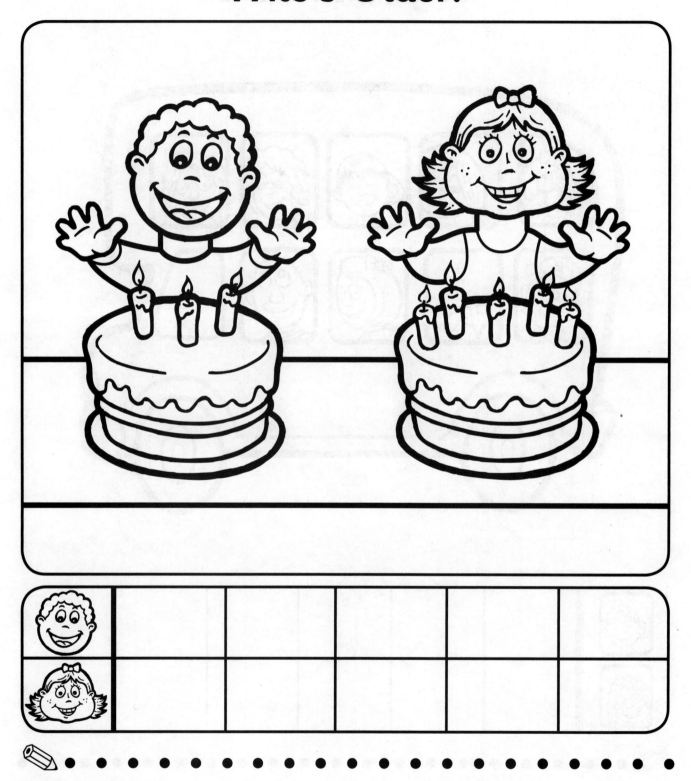

Directions: Count the candles on each birthday cake. Graph the total for each. Color the birthday cake for the older child.

Name _____

Dinner Time

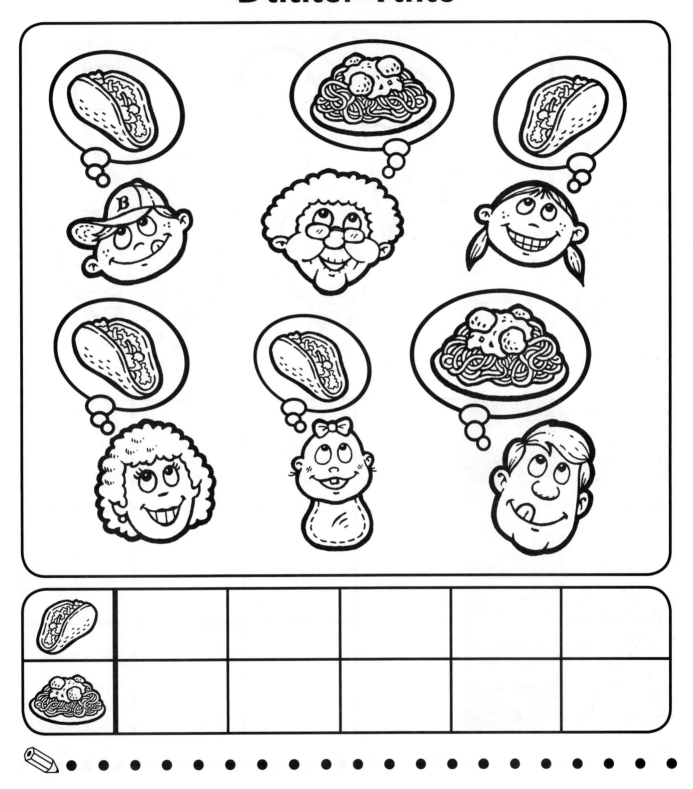

Directions: Count each type of food. Graph the total for each. Circle the row with the most popular food.

Name _____

Ice-Cream Cones

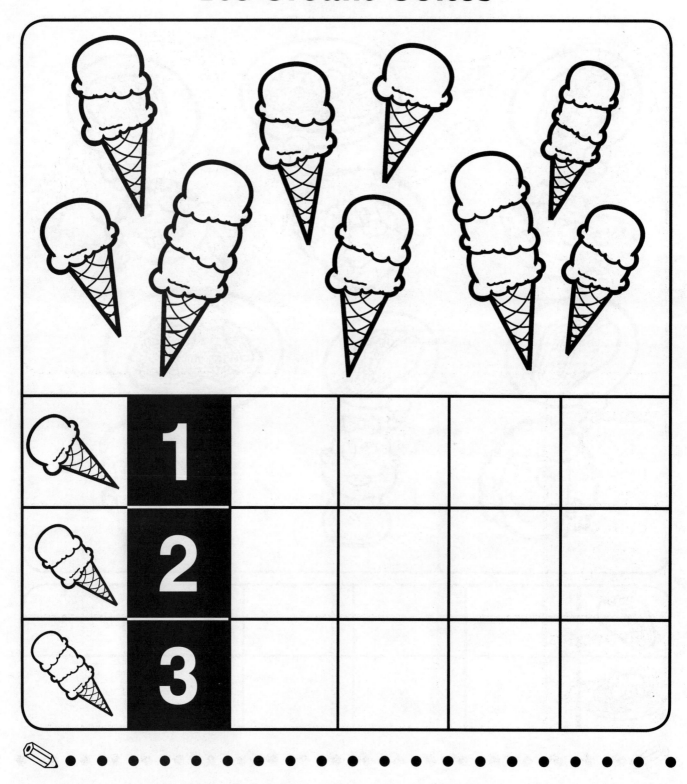

Directions: Count the scoops on each ice-cream cone. Graph the total for each type of ice-cream cone.

Name _____

Vegetable Garden

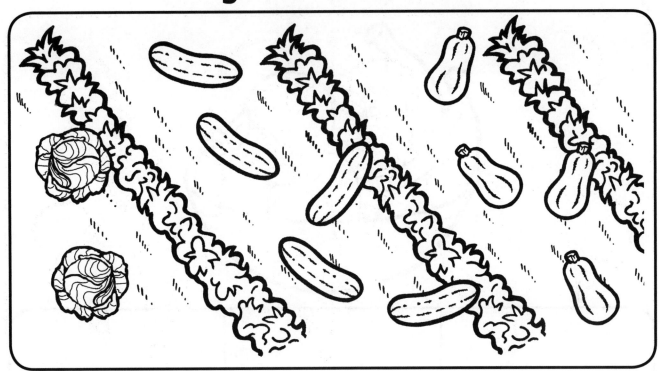

Squash					
Lettuce					
Cucumbers					

Directions: Count each type of vegetable in the garden. Graph the total for each.

Name _____

Fruit Graph

Directions: Count each type of fruit in the bowl. Graph the total for each.

Name _____

Different Dinosaurs

Directions: Count each type of dinosaur. Graph the total for each.

Name _____

Name Graph

Your Name

Your Friend's Name

Your Friend's Name

Directions: Write each letter of your name and two friends' names in the boxes. Look at the results of the graph. Circle the name that has the greatest number of letters. Draw a rectangle around the name with the fewest letters.

Name _____

Bug Graph

Ladybugs	**Caterpillars**	**Ants**

• •

Directions: Count each type of bug in the jar. Graph the total for each.

Toothbrush Count

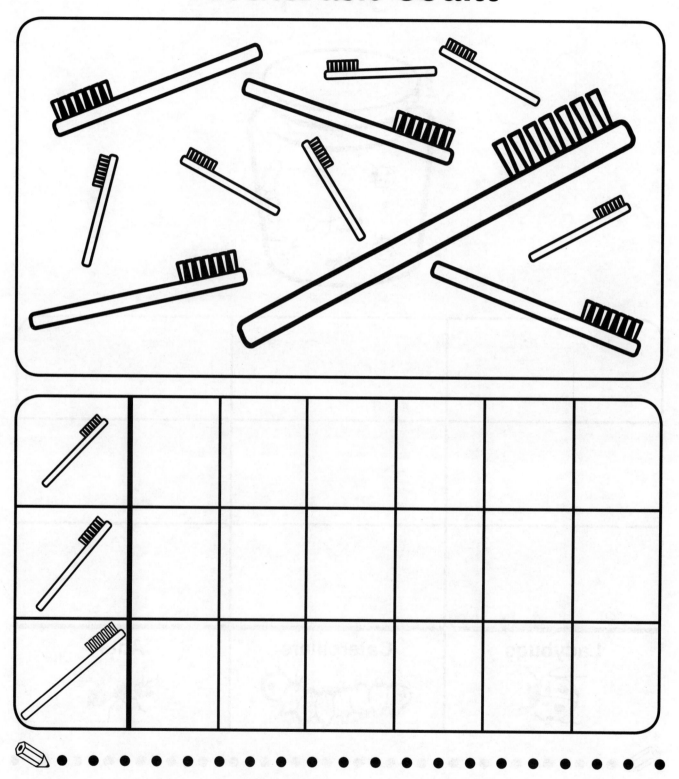

Directions: Count each size of toothbrush. Graph the total for each.

Name _____

Time To Tally

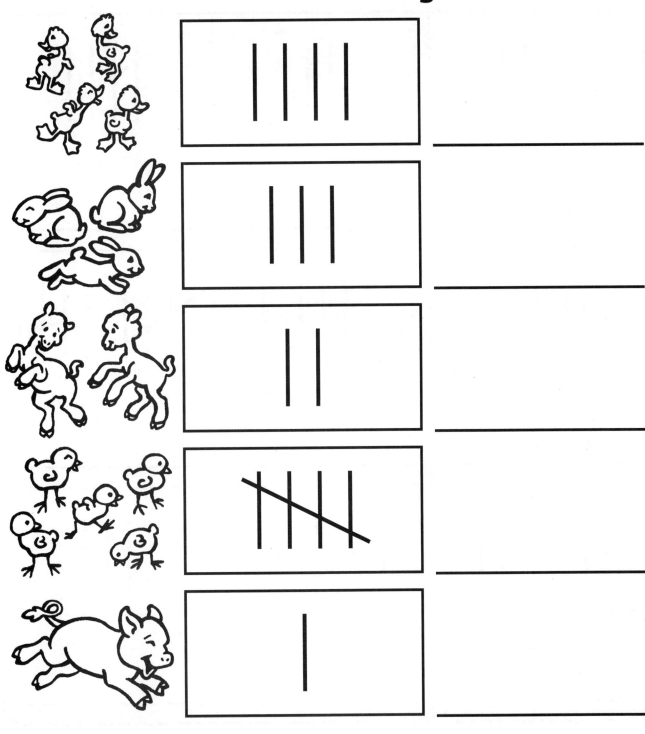

Directions: Look at the animals at the beginning of each row. Count the tally marks in each box. Write the number on the line.

Name _____

Count the Tallies

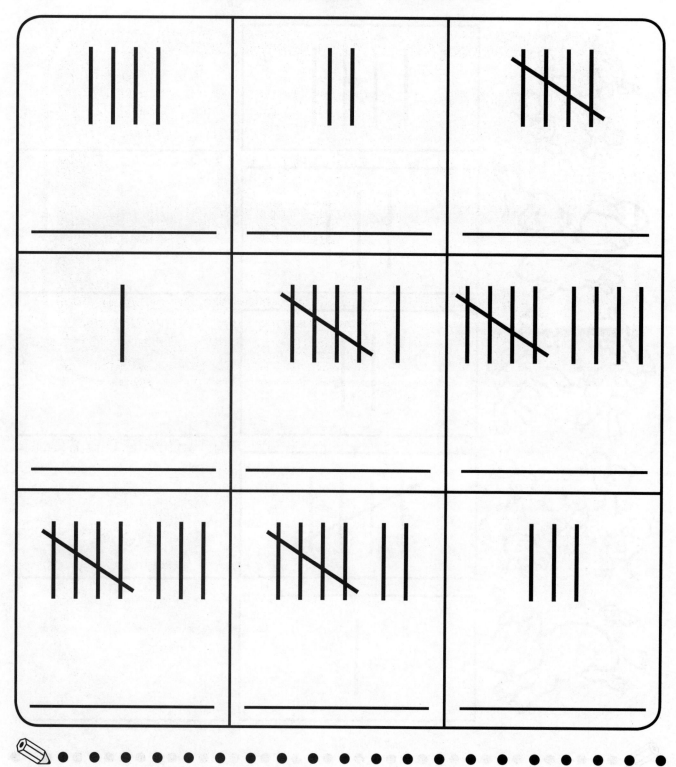

Directions: Count the tally marks in each box. Write the number on the line.

Name _____

Soccer Time

SCOREBOARD

WILDCATS |||| |

BEARS |||||

• How many goals did the Wildcats have?

• How many goals did the Bears have?

 • • • • • • • • • • • • • • • • •

Directions: Count the tally marks to see how many goals each team scored. Write the correct number of goals in each soccer ball. Circle the winning team's soccer ball.

Name _____

On the Go

Directions: Count each type of vehicle. Cut out each set of tally marks and glue it in the corresponding box.

Name _____

Number Tally

6	2
1	5
3	7
8	4

Directions: Look at the number in each box. Make the correct number of tally marks below each number.

Hotdog Contest

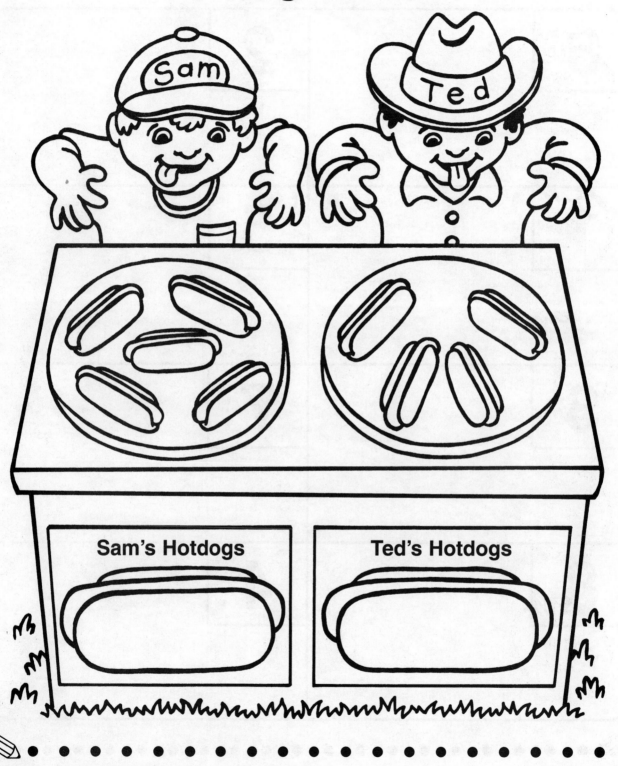

Directions: Count the hotdogs on each boy's plate. Use tally marks to show the number of hotdogs Sam plans to eat. Use tally marks to show the number of hotdogs Ted plans to eat.

Name _____

Alphabet Hunt

• •

Directions: Look at the letters on the apples. Make a tally mark next to the corresponding letter each time you find that letter.

Name _____

Ball Tally

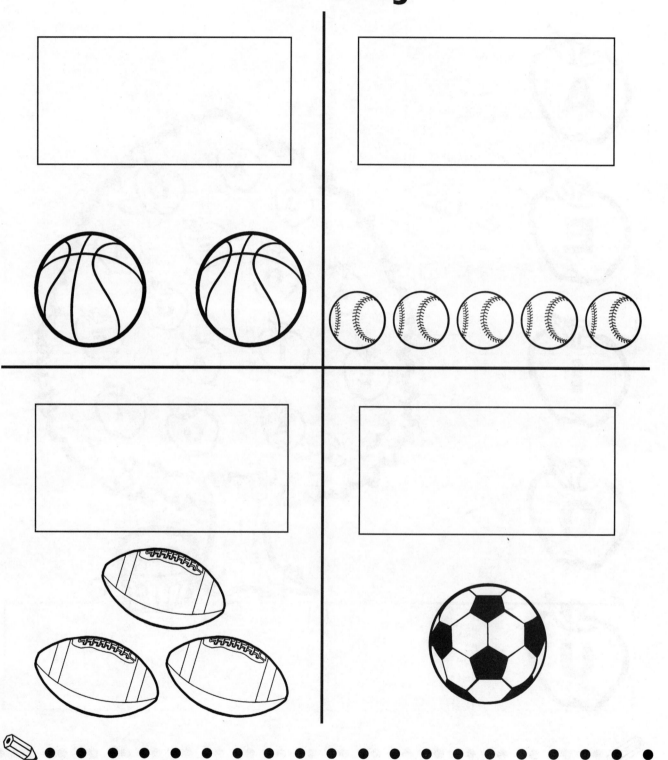

Directions: Count each type of sports ball. Use tally marks to show the number of each ball.

Name _____

Lots of Spots

Directions: Count the spots on each dog. Use tally marks to show the number of spots on each dog.

Name _____

What's the Weather?

Sunny									
Snowy									
Rainy									
Cloudy									

Directions: Look at the weather graph for March. Use tally marks to show the number of days for each type of weather.

Name _____

On a Roll

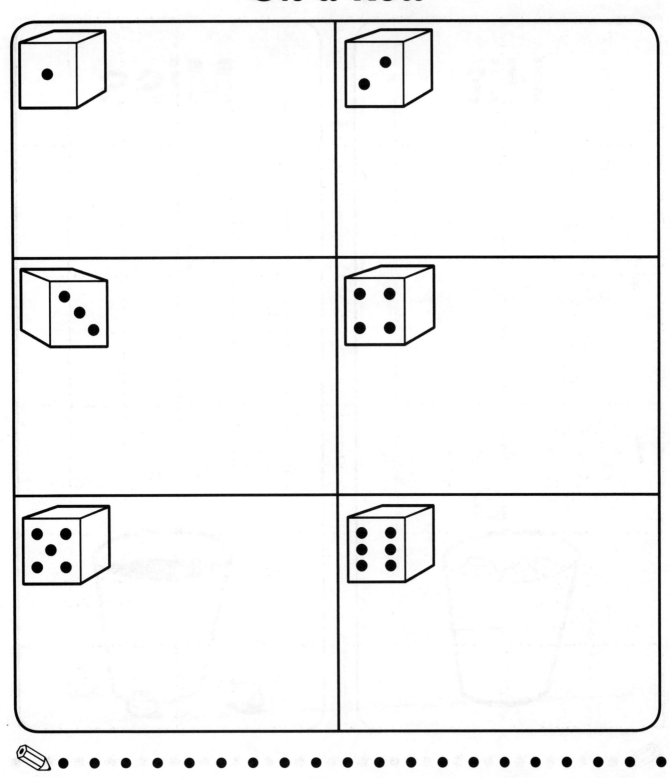

Directions: Roll a die 20 times. Make a tally mark next to each number that you roll.

Hit or Miss?

Hit	Miss

Directions: Wad a sheet of paper into a ball. Toss the ball into a bucket or container. Tally the number of times you hit and miss the bucket.